EAU CLAIRE DISTRICT LIBRARY
6528 East Main Street
P.O. Box 328
EAU CLAIRE, MI 49111

W9-ALL-908

J
363.34
Wor

WORLD BOOK'S
LIBRARY OF NATURAL DISASTERS

FLOODS

WORLD BOOK

a Scott Fetzer company
Chicago
www.worldbookonline.com

EAU CLAIRE DISTRICT LIBRARY

T 142448

8/12/08 World Book $20⁹⁰

World Book, Inc.
233 N. Michigan Avenue
Chicago, IL 60601
U.S.A.

For information about other World Book publications, visit our Web site at
http://www.worldbookonline.com or call **1-800-WORLDBK (967-5325).**

For information about sales to schools and libraries, call **1-800-975-3250 (United States);**
1-800-837-5365 (Canada).

© 2008 World Book, Inc. All rights reserved. This book may not be reproduced in whole or
in part in any form without prior written permission from the publisher.

WORLD BOOK and the GLOBE DEVICE are registered trademarks or trademarks of
World Book, Inc.

Library of Congress Cataloging-in-Publication Data
Floods.
      p. cm. -- (World Book's library of natural disasters)
    Summary: "A discussion of a major types of natural
disaster, including descriptions of some of the most
destructive; explanations of these phenomena, what
causes them, and where they occur; and information
about how to prepare for and survive these forces of
nature. Features include an activity, glossary, list of
resources, and index"--Provided by publisher.
    Includes bibliographical references and index.
    ISBN 978-0-7166-9805-0
    1. Floods--Juvenile literature.
I. World Book, Inc.
GB1399.F589 2008
363.34'93--dc22
                2007008818

World Book's Library of Natural Disasters
Set ISBN: 978-0-7166-9801-2

Printed in China
1 2 3 4 5 6 7 8 12 11 10 09 08 07

Editor in Chief: Paul A. Kobasa

Supplementary Publications
    Associate Director: Scott Thomas
    Managing Editor: Barbara A. Mayes

Editors: Jeff De La Rosa, Nicholas Kilzer,
    Christine Sullivan, Kristina A. Vaicikonis,
    Marty Zwikel

Researchers: Cheryl Graham, Jacqueline Jasek

Permissions Editor: Janet T. Peterson

Graphics and Design
    Associate Director: Sandra M. Dyrlund
    Associate Manager, Design: Brenda B. Tropinski
    Associate Manager, Photography: Tom Evans

Product development: Arcturus Publishing Limited

Writer: Chris Oxlade

Editors: Nicola Barber, Alex Woolf

Designer: Jane Hawkins

Illustrator: Stefan Chabluk

Acknowledgements:

AP Photo: cover/ title page (Wide World), 11.

Corbis: 4 (Luca Zennaro/ epa), 5, 20, 21 (Martin Bennett/ Reuters), 9 (Eric Miller/ Reuters), 10 (Adeel Halim/ Reuters),
    12 (epa), 15, 17 (Najlah Feanny), 19, 22, 31, 33 (Bettmann), 23 (Stringer/ USA/ Reuters), 25 Corbis, 27 (Shannon
    Stapleton/ Reuters), 30 (Blaine Harrington III), 34 (Julia Waterlow/ Eye Ubiquitous), 35 (Roger Wood),
    37 (T.Mughal/ epa), 39 (Joseph Sohm/ Visions of America), 41 (Reuters), 43 (Silva Joao/ Corbis Sygma).

NASA: 16 (images created by Jesse Allen, Earth Observatory, using data provided courtesy of the Landsat Project
    Science Office), 26 (image courtesy the MODIS Rapid Response Team at Goddard Space Flight Center),
    42 (Goddard Space Flight Center Scientific Visualization Studio).

Science Photo Library: 13 (NASA), 18 (David Nunuk), 28 (Gary Hincks), 36 (David Hay Jones), 40 (Paul Rapson).

Shutterstock: 29 (Norliza binti Azman).

TABLE OF CONTENTS

Glossary There is a glossary of terms on pages 45-46. Terms defined in the glossary are in type **that looks like this** on their first appearance on any spread (two facing pages).

Additional resources Books for further reading and recommended Web sites are listed on page 47. Because of the nature of the Internet, some Web site addresses may have changed since publication. The publisher has no responsibility for any such changes or for the content of cited sources.

WHAT IS A FLOOD?

Heavy rain turns the Bisagno River in Genoa, Italy, into a raging torrent in 2002. Such fast-moving floodwater can even cause bridges to collapse.

A flood is a body of water that covers normally dry ground. Most floods occur when rivers overflow. Lakes and seas may also flood low-lying **coastal plains.** Floods can bring fast-flowing, deep, dirty water, causing massive damage to property and threatening people's lives with little warning. Floods have probably killed more people than any other single type of natural disaster.

Flood hazards

The risk of drowning ranks as the most serious danger from floods. Fast-flowing water can sweep even strong swimmers into the currents and drown them. People can also be injured or killed by collisions with **debris** in the water. The water may trap people against underwater obstacles. Even shallow floodwater can carry away vehicles.

Water damages buildings in different ways. Fast-flowing torrents can topple buildings or **erode** the ground under their foundations, causing them to collapse. Wood-framed houses and other lightweight buildings may be washed away. River bridges sometimes collapse from the pressure of the floodwater flowing beneath. Floods may also undermine roads or erode their surfaces.

Buildings immersed in floodwater often suffer great damage. The water may destroy electrical systems and furnishings and leave the buildings full of mud. Floodwater can also swamp **sewerage** and water-supply systems, **contaminating** the water supply with dangerous water-borne **microorganisms,** including the bacterium that causes **cholera** *(KOL uhr uh).*

THE GREAT FLOOD

The religious traditions of many peoples include stories of great floods. The Bible tells the story of the Deluge, which covered the surface of Earth, killing all human beings except a man named Noah and his family. Some scientists believe that the story may have been inspired by a flood that occurred when the Mediterranean Sea overflowed into the Black Sea. They have found thick layers of saltwater shells that could have been left there about 7,500 years ago.

Living with floods

Millions of people live in places where they are at risk from flooding. Most live by rivers because they provide a source of water, produce good soil for farming, and serve as a means of transporting goods and materials. Many cities around the world have developed alongside large rivers.

A man inspects the damage in his house after a flash flood devastated Boscastle in the United Kingdom in 2004.

THE SCIENCE OF WATER

To understand floods, we must first understand the science of rivers and the processes that circulate water on Earth. A river carries water from the land to the sea or into a lake. A river system consists of the river and its **tributaries**—the smaller streams that feed water to the river. From high above, a river system looks like a tree with a trunk, branches, and twigs. The area of land that supplies water to a river is known as that river's **drainage basin.**

The water cycle

Water constantly moves between the seas and oceans, the **atmosphere,** and the land—a system known as the **water cycle** or hydrologic cycle. Water flowing through rivers makes up one part of the water cycle. The cycle begins as the sun's heat **evaporates** water from the seas, oceans, and land, forming **water vapor** in the air. Some of this water vapor cools and **condenses** into tiny water droplets or ice crystals that make up clouds. The water then falls as rain or snow.

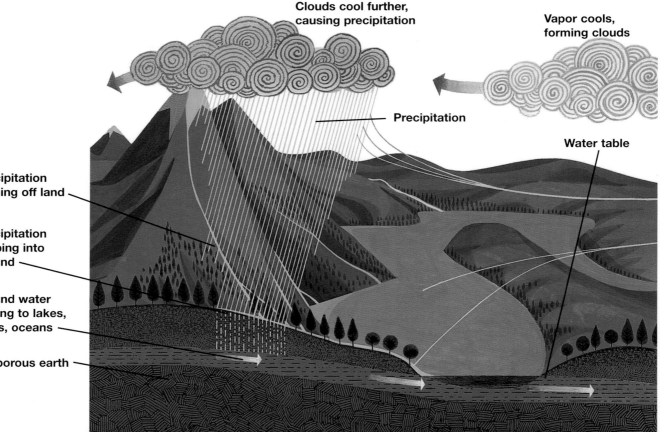

Clouds cool further, causing precipitation

Vapor cools, forming clouds

Precipitation

Water table

Precipitation running off land

Precipitation seeping into ground

Ground water flowing to lakes, rivers, oceans

Nonporous earth

Rain that falls on the land may take two forms: (1) **ground water** and (2) **surface runoff.** Ground water soaks into the ground and moves through the soil and rock. It may come out of the ground again at springs, forming streams. Surface runoff flows across the land, running downhill into streams, rivers, and lakes.

Parts of a river

River water flows along channels. The bottom of a channel is called the bed, and the sides are called the banks. A river flows from high ground—such as hills and mountains—to lower ground and, eventually, to its **mouth** at the coast or in a lake. Rivers tend to be steep and fast-flowing in their upper stages. But as the river nears its mouth, it slows as it carries a greater quantity of water through a wider and deeper channel. Wide, flat areas of land called **flood plains** run along the lower stages of some rivers. These areas become covered with water when the river overflows its banks.

LEVEES
During floods, the water deposits rock and soil on the flood plains. This **sediment** often collects on the portion of the plain near the riverbanks, making the banks stand higher than the rest of the plain. These raised banks, called natural **levees,** act as future flood protection.

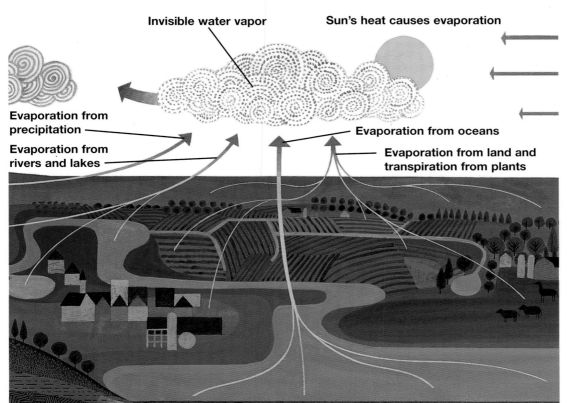

Invisible water vapor

Sun's heat causes evaporation

Evaporation from precipitation

Evaporation from rivers and lakes

Evaporation from oceans

Evaporation from land and transpiration from plants

Water is constantly moving from the seas and oceans, to Earth's atmosphere, to the land, and back to the seas and oceans again.

WHAT CAUSES FLOODS?

River floods occur when more water flows down a river than can fit into the river channel. The excess water overflows the banks and covers the **flood plain.** The most common cause of river floods is heavy rain falling over the river's **drainage basin** or snow melting within the basin.

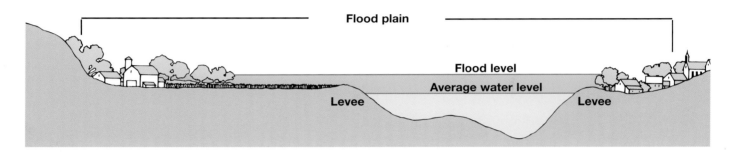

Flood plain

Flood level

Average water level

Levee   Levee

The most common type of flood occurs when a river rises above its normal level and overflows its banks. People build levees along some rivers to hold back the water, but floodwaters can overflow such barriers. Floodwaters generally cover only a river's flood plain. But sometimes extremely high waters flood a much larger area.

Sources of floodwater

River floodwater consists of **ground water** that comes out of the ground at springs, **surface runoff,** and melting ice and snow. The flow from springs increases as the ground becomes soaked, or **saturated.** When the ground becomes saturated right up to the surface, it cannot absorb more rain. As a result, the excess water forms puddles or runs off into streams. Water also runs off when the rainfall is so heavy that the soil cannot soak it up fast enough. In places where water cannot soak in or run downhill, it forms pools that flood the land.

The flood surge

As rain falls in a river's drainage basin, the flow from springs and the amount of runoff both increase, gradually raising the level of water in the river. The river may not begin to flood until many hours after the rain starts. As the rain stops, the runoff soon stops too. When all the excess ground water has flowed from the springs, the river level begins to drop again. The floodwater moves **downstream,** producing a **flood surge** that makes the water level rise and fall as it passes.

Thousands of acres of farmland in Minnesota are under water as a result of the Red River overflowing its banks in 2006.

The surge may cause flooding hundreds of miles from the original source of the floodwater. In large rivers, the flood surge can take days to reach the sea.

Coastal floods

Coastal floods happen when sea level rises above the level of low-lying **coastal plains,** also known as coastal strips. Storms cause most coastal floods. **Hurricanes** and other powerful swirling storms can produce **storm surges**—enormous rushes of seawater that may flow far inland (see page 22).

INCREASING RUNOFF

Some types of land produce more surface runoff than others and are, therefore, more likely to cause flooding. When rain batters bare soil, the force of the rain compresses the top layer of soil, making it hard and preventing water from soaking in. In urban areas, runoff is high because such surfaces as roofs, roads, and pavement do not soak up water. Trees, bushes, and other vegetation help to prevent flooding because they protect the soil and provide natural drainage.

THE MUMBAI MONSOON OF 2005

In 2005, record-breaking rainfall caused floods that brought India's largest city—Mumbai, formerly Bombay—to a standstill. The city of 12 million people and India's financial capital lies on India's west coast in the state of Maharashtra. The flooding caused widespread damage and killed more than 1,000 people.

Monsoon rains

Summer is the rainy season in many parts of India. In summer, winds called **monsoons** blow from the sea, bringing heavy rains and often causing flooding in coastal areas. The summer monsoon of 2005 led to heavy rainfalls that produced floods across many parts of India. On July 26, 2005, 37 inches (94 centimeters) of rain fell in one part of Mumbai, breaking the record for the heaviest daily rainfall in all of India. The city received half its annual rainfall in just 24 hours. In Mumbai, a high tide prevented old **storm drains** built to carry away floodwater from working properly. Two of Maharashtra's major rivers, the Godavari and the Dudhna, also flooded.

Torrential rains in July 2005 leave a Mumbai city bus stranded in knee-high flood water.

A swamped city

The floods filled one-third of Mumbai's streets with water. In some places, the water rose above people's heads. In others, the current flowed too fast to wade through. The city became gridlocked in the evening rush hour. With the roads and tracks submerged, buses and trains stopped running. The airport was forced to close as well.

People became trapped overnight on the upper floors of stores and offices. In addition, communications became difficult because telephone systems broke down. In the countryside, floods washed away thousands of residences and many roads and bridges. With the help of the Indian armed forces, at least 500,000 people were evacuated from their flooded houses. It took days to restore electric power and fresh water and clear the streets of **debris** and the bodies of dead farm animals. Further heavy rains and flooding hampered the cleanup efforts.

LANDSLIDES

Floods may produce a deadly side effect called a **landslide.** When soil on steep slopes becomes **saturated** with water, it becomes unstable and the soil can slump down the hill. During the 2005 floods in Mumbai, most of the deaths were caused by landslides, which buried hundreds of people living in shacks in the city's slums.

People struggle to hang on to a rope stretched across a flooded street in Mumbai, India, on July 27, 2005, one day after the heaviest rainfall ever recorded in India on a single day.

FLOOD PATTERNS

River floods follow a seasonal pattern because the amount of water flowing down rivers changes throughout the year. The pattern depends on the climate in the river's **drainage basin.** Places near oceans usually have a climate with more rainfall in winter than in summer, and so have an increased chance of winter floods. The middle regions of continents have higher rainfall in summer, making summer floods more likely.

Spring floods

In addition to rainfall, some rivers get water from melting snow and ice on hills and mountains. Snow and ice normally start to thaw in the spring. In high mountains, the thaw lasts into the summer. As a result, rivers that have snow-capped hills and mountains in their drainage basins are most prone to flooding in the spring and early summer.

A village in Andhra Pradesh, in southern India, is almost completely submerged by monsoon floods in 2006. The floodwaters claimed 125 victims and left an estimated 130,000 people homeless.

Monsoon floods

The **monsoons** that blow during two seasons in southern Asia can cause floods in the region. The winter monsoon blows from the northeast and brings cool, dry air; the summer monsoon blows from the southwest and brings warm, moist air from the Indian Ocean. The summer monsoon also brings heavy rain for two or three months and causes many rivers in southern Asia to flood.

The severity of floods

Some rivers flood frequently, as often as once every year. These frequent floods are usually minor and produce little damage. Floods that happen less frequently tend to be more severe and cause more destruction. **Hydrologists** *(hy DROL uh gistz),* or scientists who study water, use a scale of probability to rank the severity of a flood. A yearly flood occurs at an average rate of once per year and is relatively mild. A 10-year flood happens an average of once every 10 years and is more severe. A 100-year flood may cause extreme devastation.

The Aswan High Dam is clearly visible in the center of a satellite image of the Nile River in Egypt. The dam holds back the waters of the river (top) to form Lake Nasser (bottom), which covers an area of approximately 1,550 square miles (4,014 square kilometers).

NILE FLOODS

The Nile River ranks as the world's longest river, running north 4,160 miles (6,695 kilometers) through northeast Africa. From April to June, heavy rains in Ethiopia and southeastern Sudan flood the rivers that flow into the Nile. For thousands of years, these rains created an annual flood in the Nile Valley in Egypt, helping Egyptian farmers to grow crops alongside the river. The floods brought silt with minerals that enriched the soil, helping the crops to grow. In 1968, the vast Aswan High Dam at Aswan, Egypt, was completed. The **dam** ended the annual flood, but it and other dams built during the 1900's regulate the flow of water for irrigation.

EAU CLAIRE DISTRICT LIBRARY

THE MISSISSIPPI-MISSOURI FLOOD OF 1993

The worst floods in the United States have occurred along the Mississippi River, the Missouri River, and their many **tributaries.** The Great Flood of 1993 ranks as one of the most severe floods in U.S. history. This flood caused about $15 billion in damage, making it also one of the costliest natural disasters in U.S. history.

Water sources

The amount of water flowing down the Mississippi and Missouri rivers varies throughout the year. Much of the Missouri's water comes from melting snow in the Rocky Mountains. Most floods on the Mississippi and Missouri result when water from snowmelt combines with spring rains. On average, the Mississippi drains about 640,000 cubic feet (18,100 cubic meters) of water into the Gulf of Mexico every second.

Map showing the Mississippi River drainage basin, including the Missouri River, Yellowstone River, Snake R., Platte R., Arkansas R., Canadian R., Red River, Ohio River, Tennessee R., Cumberland R., St. Lawrence River, Colorado River, and Rio Grande. Cities labeled include Minneapolis, Milwaukee, Chicago, Omaha, Denver, Kansas City, St. Louis, Memphis, New Orleans, Louisville, Cincinnati, Pittsburgh.

Scale: 400 Miles / 400 Kilometers

Legend: Mississippi River drainage basin

The Missouri flows east from the Rocky Mountains in southwestern Montana into the Mississippi River near St. Louis, Missouri. The Mississippi flows from its source in northwestern Minnesota south to Louisiana, where it empties into the Gulf of Mexico.

Causes of the 1993 flood

The Great Flood of 1993 resulted from heavier-than-normal rainfall that lasted for several months. The heavy rains began in the spring and continued into summer with storms that dropped rain almost every day for two months; 1993 developed into the wettest summer on record in some states, with two to three times the normal rainfall. By June, the ground was **saturated,** and the rain had nowhere to go but into the rivers. The Mississippi began to flood in June and the Missouri in mid-July. In all, 150 rivers in the **drainage basin** broke their banks. The waters stayed at flood level until the middle of September. Some areas remained underwater for nearly 200 days. **Hydrologists** rank the Great Flood of 1993 as a 100-year flood.

THE MISSISSIPPI-MISSOURI RIVER SYSTEM

The Missouri and the Mississippi rank as the longest and second-longest rivers in the United States. The Mississippi-Missouri drainage basin is the third-largest in the world. It drains an area of about 1,247,300 square miles (3,243,490 square kilometers), roughly one-third the area of the United States. In its lower reaches, the Mississippi's **flood plain** measures more than 50 miles (80 kilometers) wide.

Floodwaters reach the top of a street sign in Illinois in August 1993. The Great Flood of 1993 was one of the most costly natural disasters ever to hit the United States.

The Great Flood of 1993 lasted from May to September. Flooding occurred across North Dakota, South Dakota, Nebraska, Kansas, Minnesota, Iowa, Missouri, Wisconsin, Illinois, and Indiana. The worst flooding took place near St. Louis, Missouri, where the Mississippi and the Missouri join, though flood defenses in St. Louis protected the city.

Flood damage

The water forced 75,000 people from their homes, and 50 people died in the floods. The flood affected an area of more than 400,000 square miles (1 million square kilometers). About 20 million acres (8 million hectares) of farmland were under water. Barge movements on the Missouri and Mississippi, which serve as major waterways, had to stop for two months because of the strong currents in the floodwaters, disrupting grain shipments.

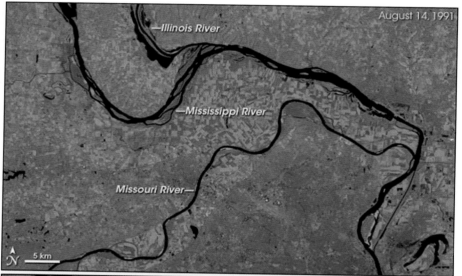

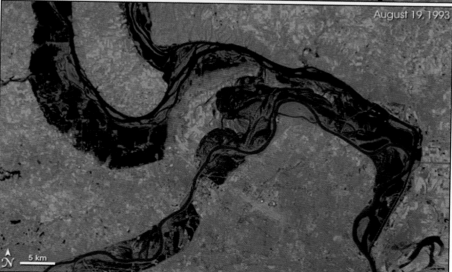

Two satellite images of the area around St. Louis, Missouri, show the Mississippi, Missouri and Illinois rivers at a normal depth (1991) and in flood (1993). Water appears dark blue, healthy vegetation is green, bare fields and freshly exposed soil are pink. The 1993 image was captured slightly after the peak water levels in this part of the Mississippi River, and the pink scars show where floodwaters have receded to leave bare land.

Levee failures

More than 1,200 artificial **levees** *(LEHV eez)* protect the **flood plains** in the Mississippi-Missouri river system. As the floodwaters approached, people built up the levees with millions of sandbags. Despite these efforts, the floodwaters broke through or poured over the top of 75 percent of the levees and spread onto the flood plain. Although most levees were rebuilt after the flood, some experts argued that the levees had actually worsened the flood by preventing water from spreading naturally over the entire flood plain.

Soldiers monitor a sandbagged levee in St. Genevieve, Missouri, in 1993. Pumps are being used to try to control floodwater levels.

Homes under siege

Jeff and Sandy Lorton owned a farm in East Hardin, Illinois, next to the Illinois River. They left their home as water flowed up the river from the flooded Mississippi, 20 miles (32 kilometers) **downstream.** Local people tried to save the farmland by building up the levee that protected it, but on July 18 the water spilled over the barrier. When Jeff Lorton visited his house by boat, the water had reached the second floor. The water did not subside until mid-August. As it did, the Lortons, like many others, had decided to build a new home on higher ground above the flood plain.

PREVIOUS FLOODS

The Mississippi River has flooded many times. While the 1993 flood was the most severe of the 1900's, highly destructive floods also occurred in 1927, 1937, 1965, 1973, 1982, and 1983. The 1927 flood lasted from March to July. It was caused by snowmelt water from the Missouri arriving at the Mississippi when it was already flooding. The floodwaters covered an area of more than 26,000 square miles (67,000 square kilometers). Some parts of the Mississippi River stretched 80 miles (130 kilometers) across and measured 100 feet (30 meters) deep.

FLASH FLOODS

Violent floods known as **flash floods** happen suddenly and last for only a short time. Flash floods are usually caused by very heavy rainfall over a small area. Such floods bring fast-flowing and destructive waters. Flash floods are also extremely dangerous because they occur with little warning.

Flash floodwater

The water that causes flash floods often comes from heavy rains produced by severe thunderstorms. These storm clouds can measure more than 9 miles (15 kilometers) high and contain millions of tons of water. They often form in summer, when the air is warm and **humid.** Such clouds produce very heavy rain and are often slow-moving, so that a great deal of rain falls in one place. Thunderclouds can collapse on themselves, releasing all their water in a short period of time in an effect known as a **cloudburst.** During a cloudburst, up to 1 inch (2.5 cm) of rain can fall in just 15 minutes. The ground cannot soak up such heavy rain, and most of the water runs off into **gullies** and streams, filling them rapidly.

A thundercloud off Easter Island in the South Pacific releases an area of intense rainfall, known as a cloudburst.

Where flash floods happen

Most flash floods happen in mountainous areas. Because rain takes the shortest route downhill, the water runs quickly into gullies and then accelerates down the mountain. A dry gully can transform into a torrent in only a few minutes. As the floodwaters pour into streams and rivers, they quickly fill up the river channels. The fast-moving water picks up soil, boulders, and such other **debris** as fallen trees. In urban areas, this debris can block **storm drains,** making the flooding worse as water is forced through streets and buildings.

No warning

The first sign of a flash flood may be the arrival of a wave of water several feet high. The depth and speed of the water causes it to push on objects with great force. Flash floodwaters can wash away cars and buildings. Debris carried along in the water can also cause damage to property or injure people caught in the floodwaters.

A rescue worker looks out for flood victims on the Big Thompson River in Colorado after a devastating flash flood in 1976. The flood swept away part of Highway 34 and drowned 139 people.

VOLCANIC FLOODS

Volcanic **eruptions** can also cause flash floods. When a high, snow-capped volcano erupts, the hot ash quickly melts large quantities of ice and snow. This water flows down the side of the volcano in torrents. The water may mix with the volcanic ash to form mudflows, called **lahars**. In 1985, lahars that formed after the eruption of Nevado del Ruiz volcano in Colombia destroyed the town of Armero, killing 23,000 people.

THE BOSCASTLE FLASH FLOOD OF 2004

In August 2004, a **flash flood** devastated the British coastal village of Boscastle, in Cornwall. Boscastle has a population of just over 800, but thousands of tourists visit every summer, and the town is full of shops and hotels. The village had been flooded many times, but the flash flood of 2004 ranked as one of the worst on record in the United Kingdom.

Local geography

Steep valleys and high **moors**—open, rolling land—surround the village of Boscastle. The lower part of the town lies in a narrow, wooded valley. The Valency River runs through the valley and into the town, where it is joined by the Jordan River, before flowing into the harbor. The area of the **drainage basins** of both rivers measures just 7.7 square miles (20 square kilometers).

Cars lie piled up on top of each other in Boscastle after the flash flood of Aug. 16, 2004.

Torrential rain

On the morning of August 16, breezes blew inland, bringing moist air from the sea. Hot sunshine and a dry breeze from the land made the moist air rise, forming a line of thunderstorms along the coast. Torrential rain began at noon and continued for five hours, drenching Boscastle and the moors north of the village. High rainfall earlier in the month had already **saturated** the ground, resulting in the water funneling down to the sea through the valleys.

Rising waters

By mid-afternoon, the Valency River had filled and began to flood the town's streets. Water swept through the tourist parking lot, carrying cars through the village and out into the harbor. A total of 115 cars were swept out to sea. The flow peaked at 5 p.m., when the water in the streets reached a depth of 10 feet (3 meters). Buildings quickly filled up with water. The water completely washed away four buildings, and trees carried by the floodwaters knocked out the walls of several others.

People inside the buildings scrambled out of skylights and onto roofs to escape the fast-rising waters. Helicopters eventually rescued about 100 people from trees, cars, and rooftops. Rescuers in boats searched for anyone who had been washed out to sea, but fortunately no one was killed. **Hydrologists** calculated that about 440 million gallons (1.7 billion liters) of water flowed through the town that afternoon and ranked the Boscastle disaster as a 400-year flood.

Two days after the flash flood, work to clean up the mess left by the floodwaters begins in Boscastle.

SWEPT AWAY

Emily Maughan lived in a house alongside the Valency River. The water broke through her front door and knocked her off her feet. "The door just flew towards me and a tidal wave of water came over the top," she later reported. Maughan was swept from her house, but she managed to grab onto a drainpipe. A neighbor heard her screams and helped her into his own flooded home.

The sea floods coastal areas when its waters rise beyond normal levels and flow across the land. Storms at sea cause most coastal floods. Other causes include extremely high tides and large waves. When storms, high tides, or large waves combine, they can produce severe coastal flooding.

Flood-risk areas

Shallow islands and low-lying coastal areas known as **coastal plains** rank as the places most at risk from sea flooding. These areas typically lie only a few feet above sea level. Much of the Atlantic Coast of the United States consists of coastal plains.

Flood water pours into a deep hole in which railroad tracks have collapsed near Zeebrugge, Belgium, in the wake of a massive 1953 storm surge off the North Sea. Triggered by severe winds, the storm surge caused widespread flooding in the United Kingdom and the Netherlands as well as Belgium.

Other countries prone to sea flooding include Belgium, where some areas lie only a few feet above sea level, and the Netherlands. Two-fifths of the Netherlands has been reclaimed from the sea and lies below sea level. Such land is often protected from flooding by sea walls or barriers. If the sea breaks through, it can cause deep flooding with water that will not naturally drain back to the sea.

Tides

Tides occur because of variations in the **gravitational** pull of the moon and the sun on different parts of Earth. These variations, combined with the rotation of the planet, cause the water level at any one place in Earth's oceans to rise and fall in cycles. Sometimes the gravitational *(GRAV uh TAY shuh nuhl)* pull of the moon and the sun work with low **atmospheric pressure** and the ocean's waves to create extremely high tides that can cause coastal flooding.

Storm surges

Swirling storm systems called **cyclones** can cause severe flooding along coasts. Within a cyclone, the atmospheric pressure at Earth's surface is lower than normal. As a result, the surface of the sea can rise. When a cyclone crosses a coast, the raised surface can produce a giant onrush of seawater known as a **storm surge** that can push far inland. Strong winds in the cyclone stir up large waves, which can worsen the flooding. The most powerful cyclones may cause storm surges measuring more than 20 feet (6 meters) tall.

BANGLADESH FLOODS

A large part of Bangladesh consists of the **deltas** of the Padma (or Ganges) River and other large rivers. Millions of people farm the low-lying islands in these deltas. Storm surges caused by **tropical cyclones** often bring terrible floods to Bangladesh. In 1970, a cyclone and storm surge killed more than 260,000 people and destroyed the homes of millions more.

Huge waves crash onto the shore of the island of Bermuda as Hurricane Fabian hits the Caribbean in 2003.

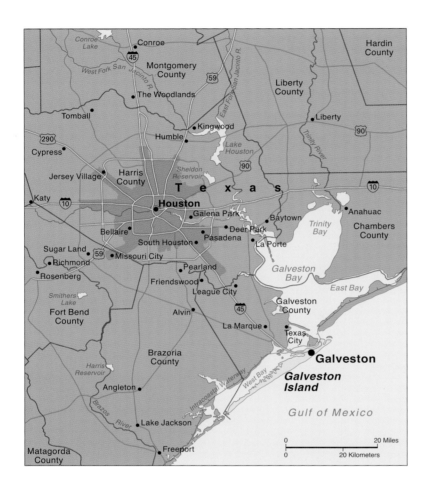

Galveston Island lies off the coast of Texas, in the Gulf of Mexico.

The city of Galveston, Texas, is a seaport on the Gulf of Mexico. On Sept. 8, 1900, a **hurricane** and **storm surge** flooded most of the city. More than 6,000 of Galveston's population of 37,800 died. The flood remains the deadliest single natural disaster in U.S. history.

The hurricane

The city of Galveston lies on Galveston Island, a long, thin, sandy stretch of land about 2 miles (3 kilometers) off the coast of Texas. In 1900, much of the island lay just 5 feet (1.5 meters) above sea level, and the city lacked any sea defenses. The storm that hit Galveston was a powerful Category 4 hurricane, the second-highest intensity level on the Saffir-Simpson hurricane rating scale. The low **atmospheric pressure** in the hurricane's central **eye** created a storm surge with waves measuring up to 15 feet (4.5 meters) high. The hurricane roared across the Gulf of Mexico and straight over Galveston Island.

Warnings ignored

Galveston's authorities knew of the approaching storm, but they didn't know exactly when it would arrive or how powerful it would be. They advised people to leave the island for higher ground, but most people ignored the warnings. On September 8, the winds gradually increased, and the atmospheric pressure dropped. The sea rose higher until it flooded Galveston's streets. By the time people tried to escape, the waters had flooded the bridge between the island and the mainland. In the early evening, fierce winds tore across the island, and huge waves swept ashore, breaking up wooden buildings and washing people away. The storm destroyed more than 3,600 houses, half of those in the city. Today, Galveston is defended by a sea wall, which saved it from flooding when hurricanes struck again in 1915, 1961, and 1983.

LOST FOREVER

Isaac M. Cline worked for the Weather Bureau in Galveston and wrote a detailed report of the disaster. He sheltered dozens of people in his home until it collapsed. His report states, "At 8:30 p.m. my residence went down with about 50 persons who had sought it for safety, and all but 18 were hurled into eternity. Among the lost was my wife, who never rose above the water after the wreck of the building."

Men use ropes to pull away the debris of ruined houses in Galveston to look for bodies after the hurricane of 1900.

HURRICANE KATRINA AND NEW ORLEANS, 2005

On Aug. 29, 2005, the city of New Orleans, Louisiana, suffered severe flooding when **Hurricane** Katrina slammed into the Gulf Coast of the United States. The hurricane's **storm surge** pushed water over and through the city's flood defenses. More than 1,500 people died in Louisiana, most from New Orleans, because they could not escape the rising waters.

Surrounded by water

New Orleans is almost completely surrounded by water. The Mississippi River runs through the city, and Lake Ponchartrain lies to the north and links to the sea. Several canals run into the city from the river and lake. A system of **levees** was designed to prevent water from flowing into the city, much of which lies below sea level.

Meteorologists ranked Hurricane Katrina as a Category 3 hurricane. The low **atmospheric pressure** under the storm and wind gusts of more than 125 miles (200 kilometers) per hour produced storm surges up to 29 feet (9 meters) high. The surges pushed water up the city's canals. Floodwaters poured over the top of the city's levees and broke through its defenses in several places.

A satellite view of Katrina over the Gulf of Mexico on Aug. 28, 2005, a day before the hurricane devastated New Orleans.

Flood effects

The flood submerged about 80 percent of the city. Tens of thousands of mostly poor and elderly people, who could not get out of the city, were trapped. Some climbed into their attic but drowned when the water rose above their roof. Others died in hospitals and nursing homes left without power and running water. In some areas, the floodwater mixed with gasoline, dead animals, mud, and other **debris,** creating a stinking liquid that rose up to 20 feet (6 meters) high. The hurricane devastated other parts of the coastlines of Alabama, Mississippi, and Louisiana, leveling some towns completely. The death toll from the storm exceeded 1,800 people.

RESCUE AND AFTERMATH

Many of the people stranded in New Orleans were trapped on rooftops and highway overpasses and in the city's convention center and sports stadium. Three days passed before the National Guard began a major rescue effort.
In September, the U.S. House of Representatives released a report that criticized federal and local officials for their lack of communication and slow response to the disaster and for failing to properly maintain the levee system.

While a house burns out of control, a firefighter struggles through the floodwaters that fill the streets of New Orleans in the aftermath of Hurricane Katrina in 2005.

TSUNAMI FLOODING

Some coastal floods result from **tsunamis** *(tsoo NAH meez).* A tsunami is a series of powerful waves caused by such events as **earthquakes, landslides,** or volcanic **eruptions.** A tsunami can travel thousands of miles across an ocean before surging onto land and flooding **coastal plains.**

How tsunamis travel

A tsunami is created by a large movement of the seabed or coastal landscape. Its waves travel away from their source in all directions, like ripples on a pond. In the deep ocean, each tsunami wave may measure just 3 feet (1 meter) in height, but they can be so long that they take more than one hour to pass by. Such waves may travel at speeds of up to 600 miles (970 kilometers) per hour. When the waves reach shallow coastal water, they slow down and "pile up," becoming at least several times taller. Tsunami waves have been known to reach heights greater than 100 feet (30 meters) above sea level. The first sign of an approaching tsunami is often the sudden outflow of ocean water, as if the tide had gone out in just a few minutes.

Out at sea, tsunami waves are so low that people aboard ships may not even notice them. But when the waves reach shallow coastal areas, they become much bigger and can be very destructive.

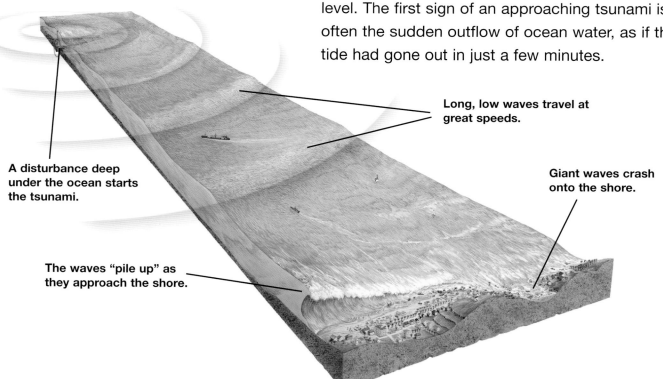

Long, low waves travel at great speeds.

A disturbance deep under the ocean starts the tsunami.

Giant waves crash onto the shore.

The waves "pile up" as they approach the shore.

Tsunami damage

When a tsunami reaches shore, its waves break and sweep onto land. Tsunami waves hit coasts at speeds of about 20 to 30 miles (30 to 50 kilometers) per hour, knocking over trees and buildings and sweeping away the **debris.** The water can then travel more than ⅔ mile (1 kilometer) inland, submerging everything. The waves can drown people or sweep them up and carry them out to sea.

Fifteen minutes after the earthquake in December 2004, powerful tsunami waves devastated much of Aceh, on the Indonesian island of Sumatra.

THE TSUNAMI OF 2004

On the morning of Dec. 26, 2004, a powerful earthquake near the island of Sumatra in Indonesia set off a tsunami that traveled across the Indian Ocean. Waves measuring up to 50 feet (15 meters) high hit the coastlines of Indonesia, Thailand, Sri Lanka, and India. Most of the affected areas had no warning of the disaster. Some experts estimate that it left more than 230,000 people dead. The waves destroyed thousands of buildings and carried away boats and vehicles. The tsunami completely wiped out some towns and villages.

DAM FLOODS

A **dam** is a barrier built across a river to obstruct the flow of water. The lake formed behind a dam is called a **reservoir.** Dams are built to store water for residences and industry, to provide water for **irrigation,** and to generate **hydroelectric power.** Dams are also designed to prevent flooding (see page 36), but they have caused floods, too. If a dam collapses, water released from the reservoir rushes into the valley below, creating a devastating **flash flood.**

Why dams collapse

Most dams consist of strong walls made from earth, rock, or concrete. These structures can be damaged by **earthquakes,** which can be triggered by water in a newly filled reservoir pressing down on the rock beneath a dam. If the dam wall is weakened, the massive push of water on the back of the dam can break it apart. In 1979, a dam on the Machu River in India collapsed during an earthquake, killing at least 5,000 people.

An aerial view of the Hoover Dam and Lake Mead on the border of Nevada and Arizona. Dams must be strong enough to withstand the pressure exerted by massive amounts of water.

A dam may also collapse if reservoir water flows over its top. The movement of the water down the front face of a dam can cause erosion, weakening the dam's wall or its foundations. Poor design can also cause dam collapses. In 1928, the St. Francis Dam near Los Angeles collapsed as its reservoir filled for the first time. Several towns below the dam were swamped, and about 500 people died. The collapse resulted from last-minute changes to the structure, including raising the height of the dam by 20 feet (6 meters). In addition, the dam was built with poor materials, which caused cracks to appear even before the reservoir was filled to capacity.

Floods caused by the intentional destruction of dams have been used as weapons of war. In 1938, the Chinese army smashed **levees** on the Huang He (Yellow River) to repel an invasion by the Japanese. During World War II (1939-1945), British bombers destroyed two German dams, causing flooding in the Ruhr industrial area of Germany.

The ruins of the St. Francis Dam near Los Angeles after the dam collapsed in 1928, releasing 12 billion gallons (45 billion liters) of water.

MANAGING WATER

The engineers who operate dams normally try to capture floodwater. But when the flow of water into a reservoir is very high, engineers can have difficultly managing all the water. If the water threatens to overtop the dam, engineers may release water from the reservoir, which can cause flooding **downstream.** In Nigeria, more than 1,000 people died and about 1,500 homes were destroyed in 1999 after emergency releases of water from three dams on the Niger River.

THE JOHNSTOWN FLOOD OF 1889

In 1889, Johnstown, Pennsylvania, was an industrial city with a population of about 30,000 people. On May 31 of that year, heavy rains caused the nearby **dam** of the South Fork Reservoir to collapse, flooding the city and other nearby towns.

A dam in disrepair

Johnstown lies at the bottom of the valley of the Little Conemaugh River. The South Fork Dam stood at the top of the valley, about 12 miles (19 kilometers) east of Johnstown. The dam consisted of an earth-and-rock embankment 72 feet (22 meters) high and 918 feet (280 meters) long. In 1889, the dam stood in a state of disrepair, with its **outlet** pipes closed and its **spillway**—the ramp that releases excess water—blocked by **debris.**

In the days before the flood, several inches (centimeters) of rain fell in the hills around the dam. The **reservoir** *(REHZ uhr vwahr)* filled quickly, but the water could not escape because of the blocked

The valley of the Little Conemaugh River, Pennsylvania, was the scene of a massive flood in 1889.

United States

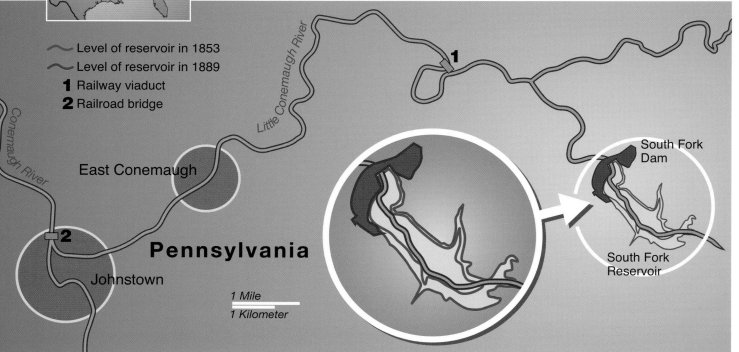

~ Level of reservoir in 1853
~ Level of reservoir in 1889
1 Railway viaduct
2 Railroad bridge

Conemaugh River

Little Conemaugh River

East Conemaugh

Pennsylvania

Johnstown

1 Mile
1 Kilometer

South Fork Dam

South Fork Reservoir

spillway. On the morning of May 31, workers tried to unblock the spillway and make the dam higher—but it was too late. Water flowed over the top of the dam, and the structure collapsed in the afternoon.

Flood effects

When the dam broke, a wall of water towering 75 feet (23 meters) high and spreading across ½ mile (0.8 kilometer) swept down the valley, picking up such debris as trees and buildings. The debris piled up against a railway viaduct, blocking the flow of water for a few minutes. When the viaduct finally collapsed under the weight of the water and debris, the wall of water rushed on, destroying the towns surrounding Johnstown. In the process, several railway locomotives—each one weighing 85 tons (77 metric tons)—were carried away. The flood hit Johnstown 57 minutes after the dam broke. The debris piled up against the town's railroad bridge, forming a mound up to 50 feet (15 meters) deep and covering about 30 acres (12 hectares). Broken oil lamps and the remains of coal fires set the mound on fire. Hundreds of people died in this wreckage. In all, the flood killed more than 2,000 people.

SURVIVOR'S STORY

Charles and Edith Richwood were riding aboard a train near East Conemaugh, Pennsylvania, on the day of the Johnstown flood. Charles Richwood later said that he "beheld a seething, turbulent wall of water whose crests seemed mountain-high." The water submerged their train, but they managed to escape and climbed onto a raft of debris with about 20 other people. They jumped off as the raft approached a wrecked and steaming ironworks and were rescued.

A house rests on its side with the trunk of a fully grown tree extending through an upper window after both were upended by the tremendous power of the 1889 Johnstown flood.

CHANGING THE ENVIRONMENT

River floods **erode** the landscape in some places by washing away soil and build it up in other places by depositing soil. These changes have useful and harmful effects on the people who live in the environment.

THE HUANG HE

The Huang He (Yellow River) is China's second-longest river. It gets its name from the huge quantities of yellow earth that it carries. The deposited sediment raises the river's bed, causing the river to change course often, which produces frequent floods. In 1887, nearly 1 million people died in the worst Huang He flood, when the river swamped an area of about 50,000 square miles (130,000 square kilometers). People sometimes call the Huang He "China's sorrow" because of the massive suffering caused by its floods.

Erosion

Erosion is a process that wears away the landscape. Rivers erode the ground by breaking up rocks and soils, forming **sediment** that flows with the water. Sediment carried along by the water is called a **load.** The load includes particles of many sizes. Larger particles of rock bump along the riverbed, increasing erosion by loosening material in the river's bed and banks. Rivers constantly erode, but a flood greatly accelerates the erosion. Floodwater carries a huge load of sediment, which makes the water muddy. Floods also cause erosion that may undermine the foundations of buildings, roads, and railroads.

Water from the Huang He (Yellow River) laden with mud and silt flows through an irrigation canal in northern China.

Deposition

The slower river water flows, the less load it can carry along. As a
river slows, its load settles to the riverbed, a process called
deposition. Deposition builds up layers of sediment on riverbeds
and **flood plains,** forms islands in rivers, and creates low-lying land
called **deltas** where rivers meet the sea. During floods, severe
erosion and deposition can dramatically change the shape of river
islands and deltas and can even permanently change the course of
a river. Deposition on flood plains helps farmers because the
sediment contains minerals that help crops to grow. Farmers in
Bangladesh tolerate regular flooding because the floods deposit
sediment that fertilizes the soil. However, deposition can also
destroy existing crops.

Floods cover farmland
near the Buriganga
River in Bangladesh.
Such floods may
deposit sediment that
fertilizes the soil.

FLOOD CONTROL

Engineers use several different methods to try to prevent flooding alongside rivers and on coasts. Such techniques range from building such massive structures as **dams** to excavating channels designed to divert the flow of water. On many rivers, engineers use a combination of methods to create an overall flood-control scheme.

A levee on the bank of the Ohio River, at the point where it meets the Mississippi River at Cairo, Illinois, safeguards the town from flood waters. During a flood, the boat launch gate in the levee is closed.

Levees

A **levee** is a natural or artificial raised riverbank. Engineers build artificial levees to keep floodwater in a river channel. Levees are constructed mostly of sandbags and earth. The Mississippi River has about 2,200 miles (3,500 kilometers) of levees that measure up to 30 feet (9.1 meters) high.

Dams

Dams provide a useful tool for controlling floods. They store in their **reservoirs** water that could cause floods **downstream** and then release the water slowly through **outlets**—giant pipes through or around the dam. Large rivers may have many dams along them to

store huge quantities of floodwater. If a reservoir becomes too full, the excess water is released through a **spillway** in a controlled flow, preventing overflows that could cause dam failures (see page 30).

Excess water is released down the spillway of the Rawal Dam near Islamabad, Pakistan, to prevent flooding after heavy monsoon rains.

Rerouting water

Engineers also prevent river floods by removing some of the water from the river. To do so, they cut a channel leading from the river to a storage pool, where water can lie until a flood surge has passed. Channels are also cut to straighten out rivers, which may allow floodwater to flow more efficiently to the sea.

Sea defenses

Sea walls, structures called **dikes,** and other barriers protect low-lying coastal land from high tides and **storm surges.** Sea walls with gates protect coastal river valleys called **estuaries** *(EHS chu EHR eez).* If a high tide or storm surge threatens to move up the estuary and flood the land on either side, the gates are closed. In the Netherlands, a network of dikes and sea walls known as the Deltaworks protects low-lying coastal areas.

FLOODWAYS

Some experts believe that the safety hazards created by dams and levees outweigh their benefits. They argue that protecting **flood plains** only encourages people to build in flood-prone areas, creating more potential for disaster when flood defenses do fail. Where towns and cities already lie along rivers, planners leave strips of farmland or parkland called **floodways** alongside the water to allow for natural flooding without damage to property.

TENNESSEE VALLEY FLOOD CONTROL

The Tennessee River begins at Knoxville, Tennessee, and flows for 650 miles (1,040 kilometers) before joining the Ohio River, near the point where the Ohio flows into the Mississippi. Floodwaters on the Tennessee River are controlled by a system of **dams** operated by the Tennessee Valley Authority (TVA). These dams also remove rapids and make waters deeper, allowing boats to navigate the river; generate **hydroelectric power;** and provide water supplies and lakes for recreation.

The Tennessee Valley Authority (TVA) is a federal corporation, established in 1933, that built a system of 39 dams on the Tennessee River and its branches to provide flood control, electric power, water recreation, and navigable waterways. In the late winter and early spring flood season, TVA lowers water levels in the lakes to create space for the expected floodwaters.

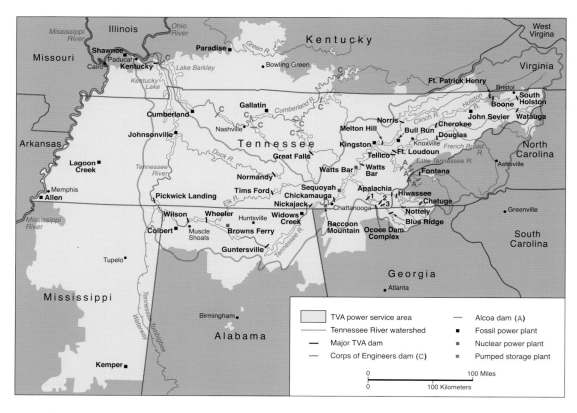

Previous floods on the Tennessee

Before all 39 TVA dams were completed, flooding was a major problem in the Tennessee Valley. Floods affected many towns and cities along the river and washed away valuable agricultural soils. Chattanooga, Tennessee, was regularly flooded because floodwater could not flow quickly enough through a valley **downstream** from the city. A disastrous flood of the river in 1937 left 500 people dead and displaced 750,000 others.

The TVA system

Assembly of the TVA system began in 1933. The system incorporated existing dams and built new facilities on the Tennessee River and its **tributaries. Upstream** of Chattanooga, at least one dam controls the water on each main tributary. Together, these dams prevent flooding at Chattanooga. Six dams lie on the Tennessee River downstream from Chattanooga, including the largest of the TVA dams— the Kentucky Dam. All of these dams can reduce the amount of water flowing into the Mississippi when it is flooding.

Operating the system

Operators carefully control the water level in the system's **reservoirs** to preserve enough storage space for floodwater. The main flood season occurs from December to May because the area experiences the heaviest rains during this period. Between July and December, operators release water from the different reservoirs to make space for the flood season. This measure provides storage for 3.3 billion gallons (12.5 billion cubic meters) of floodwater across the whole system. When the river flow subsides, operators slowly release the stored floodwater. After the flood season, they allow the reservoirs to fill again to store water for domestic supply and to generate electric power.

TVA SUCCESSES

The TVA flood-control system has worked as planned to prevent flooding. The dams saved Chattanooga from severe flooding by lowering the water level in the Tennessee by 22 feet (6.7 meters) in 1957 and by 15 feet (4.6 meters) in 1973. In 1958, the system prevented the Mississippi River from flooding at Cairo, Illinois. Today, experts estimate that the TVA prevents an average of $224-million worth of flood damage each year in the Tennessee Valley and along the Ohio and Mississippi rivers.

A barge moves through one of the giant canal locks in the Kentucky Dam, a TVA facility on the Tennessee River.

FLOOD PREDICTION AND RESCUE

Flood forecasting can reduce danger to people and property by accurately predicting when and where floods might occur. Forecasts allow authorities to activate flood protection systems, build temporary flood defenses, and conduct evacuations in time. However, even when warnings are given, many people can still be caught in floods. These people then have to be rescued.

Forecasting and monitoring

The first stage in flood prediction involves forecasting the likelihood of large quantities of rainfall. Forecast reports are then passed to the authorities monitoring rivers, who use them to predict how the rain will affect water levels and whether it will produce floods. To make their predictions, **hydrologists** consider previous rainfall and flood records and use computer simulations of a river's **drainage basin.** Rain gauges measure how much rain actually falls, so that predictions can be constantly updated. Gauging stations along rivers measure water levels, providing continuous tracking of floodwater.

A hydrologist adjusts a water gauge in a river. The level of the water is recorded by the movement of a pen across a chart drum.

Predicting coastal floods

Meteorologists *(MEE tee uh ROL uh jists)* track storms by satellite to help them predict where weather systems will hit islands and coasts. However, storms can change direction suddenly, making accurate forecasting difficult at times. Meteorologists can predict the height of a **storm surge** based on measurements of the **atmospheric pressure** inside the storm, the strength of its winds, and the height of the tides. Forecasters use this information to calculate the possibility of flooding in a particular area. **Tsunami** warning systems detect **earthquakes** and measure sea levels to give warnings of approaching tsunamis. Complex warning systems monitor the Pacific Ocean, areas of the Indian Ocean, and the waters around Japan.

Rescue and aid

Once floodwaters start to rise, emergency services personnel search for people in the water or those trapped on high ground or in cars, buildings, or trees. Rescuers may use helicopters to save people in immediate danger from rising or fast-flowing water. Flood evacuees need temporary shelter, food, and water. Where homes have been destroyed, communities need long-term aid for rebuilding.

Rescue workers search the flooded streets of Bitterfeld, Germany, for stranded people after torrential rains in August 2002.

FLOOD ALERTS

When flooding appears likely along a river or on a coast, authorities may issue flood alerts on the radio, on television, and on the Internet. They may provide different levels of alerts depending on the possibility of flooding. For example, in the United States, a *flood watch* means that rain may be heavy enough to lead to flooding; a *flood warning* means that serious flooding will soon begin or has already happened.

DISASTER AND RESCUE IN MOZAMBIQUE, 2000

Heavy rains and a **cyclone** led to floods that swamped a wide area of southern Africa in February and March 2000. Mozambique, which lies on Africa's southeast coast, suffered its worst flooding in 50 years. Thousands of people were rescued from the waters, and hundreds of thousands needed long-term aid. Mozambique required international assistance because the disaster was too large for the country to cope with alone.

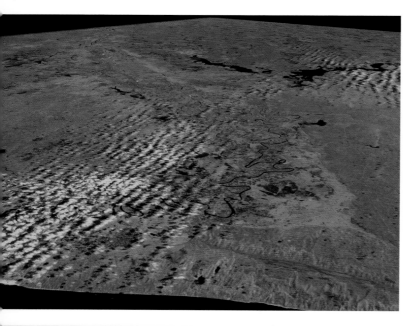

Rainfall and flash floods

In February 2000, weeks of heavy rain caused flooding on several rivers in southern and central Mozambique, including the Save and Limpopo. The disaster worsened with the arrival of Cyclone Eline on February 22, causing **flash floods.** In many areas, the water rose from 20 to 26 feet (6 to 8 meters) above normal levels.

About 700 people died in the floods. Small-scale farmers suffered great losses, with 371,000 acres (150,000 hectares) of crops covered with water, nearly one-third of all cattle drowned, and irrigation systems badly damaged. Floods and power outages forced many factories to shut down, causing serious harm to the country's economy.

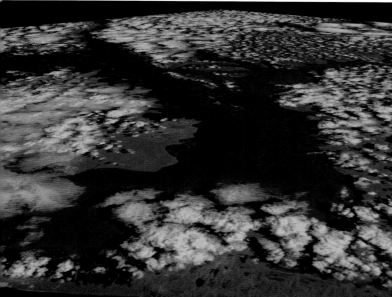

Two computer images compiled from satellite data contrast Mozambique in 1999 (top) and after the terrible floods of February 2000 (bottom).

Rescue and aid

A lack of rescue equipment delayed early rescue efforts. Mozambique's navy supplied some small boats and South Africa loaned a dozen helicopters. It took many days before rescue equipment from European countries and the United States arrived. In all, some 45,600 people were rescued from trees, roofs, and remote areas of high ground. About 1 million people needed shelter, clean water, food, and medical supplies. The United Nations and such international aid agencies as Oxfam boosted Mozambique's aid effort. Together these organizations set up more than 100 aid camps and distributed supplies by truck, boat, and helicopter. In the months after the flood, aid agencies helped people to set up new homes, restore water supplies and sanitation, and plant new crops. Much of the equipment they supplied helped Mozambique to cope with further flooding in 2001.

Residents of Palmeira in Mozambique wade through rising waters to safety during the floods of February 2000.

SEPARATED FAMILIES

The floodwaters drove in rapidly, and many families were split up as they swam for high ground or clung to trees and buildings. Thousands of children arrived alone in emergency camps and did not see their parents for days or weeks. Many people refused to go to camps and instead went to search for their missing relatives. Such agencies as Save the Children worked hard to help reunite families.

ACTIVITY

EROSION AND FLOOD DEPOSITION

Equipment

- A large plastic plate with a rim
- A small plastic tray
- Sand
- A plastic pitcher

Do this project outdoors because you may spill water and sand.

1. Spread sand on the large plate until it forms a layer about $^1/_2$ inch (1 centimeter) deep all over the plate. If the sand is dry, add a little water to help it stick together.

2. Put a piece of wood or a block under one end of the plate to make the plate slant.

3. Place the small tray at the lower end of the plate.

4. Slowly pour water from the pitcher into the sand at the high end of the plate and watch what happens to the water and sand. The water **erodes** the sand like a river eroding its banks.

5. If you pour the water much faster, the erosion increases, just as floods cause greater erosion. The sand is carried along in the water.

6. The water spills out onto the small tray and deposits the sand. This is what happens when muddy floodwater spreads out onto a **flood plain,** depositing **sediment** that makes soil fertile.

atmosphere The layer of gases surrounding Earth.

atmospheric pressure The weight of the air pressing down on Earth's surface.

cholera A water-borne disease caused by bacteria.

cloudburst A sudden, intense rainfall over a small area.

coastal plains Low-lying coastal land areas.

condense To change from a gas to a liquid as a result of cooling.

contaminate To pollute water or another substance with such dangerous materials as chemicals or bacteria.

cyclone In the tropics, a violent, swirling storm with high winds and heavy rainfall.

dam A barrier built to restrict the flow of a river and to store water.

debris Rubble, broken objects, and other damaged material.

delta The fan-shaped area at the mouth of some rivers, where the main flow splits into smaller channels.

deposition The process by which rivers deposit layers of sediment on the riverbed, on flood plains, and in deltas.

dike A bank, often made of earth, built as a defense against flooding.

downstream Down a river, toward the sea.

drainage basin The area of land drained by a river.

earthquake A shaking of the ground caused by the sudden movement of underground rock.

erode To wear away by the movement of water or winds.

eruption The pouring out of gases, lava, and rocks from a volcano.

estuary A mouth of a river that forms a valley at a coast.

evaporate To change from a liquid into a vapor.

eye The calm area at the center of a hurricane.

flash flood A sudden, intense flood of a river or lake.

flood plain The flat area of land alongside a river that can become covered with water when the river floods.

flood surge The surge of water that moves down a river during a flood, making the water level rise and fall as it passes each place on the river.

floodway A natural or artificial strip of land on a flood plain that allows floodwater to spread out naturally.

gravitational Related to gravity, the effect of a force of attraction that acts between objects because of their mass—that is, the amount of matter the objects have.

ground water Water held beneath Earth's surface.

gully A small, steep-sided valley

humid Describes air that contains a high amount of moisture (water vapor).

hurricane A tropical storm over the North Atlantic Ocean, the Caribbean Sea, the Gulf of Mexico, or the Northeast Pacific Ocean.

hydroelectric power Electric power produced using the energy of flowing water.

hydrologist A scientist who studies water.

irrigation The watering of land by artificial means.

lahar A volcanic mudflow, made up of water and ash.

landslide A mass of soil and rock that slides down a slope.

levee An embankment or wall built to prevent flooding.

load The material, such as sediment, carried along by a river.

microorganism A living thing too small to be seen except with a microscope.

monsoon A wind that reverses itself seasonally, especially the one that blows across the Indian Ocean and surrounding land areas.

moor Open, rolling land.

mouth The end of a river—where it meets the sea, another river, or another body of water.

outlet A giant pipe through or around a dam through which water is released from the reservoir.

reservoir A place, such as the space behind a dam, where water is collected and stored for use.

saturate To soak completely.

sediment Particles of earth, rock, or other matter carried along or deposited by water.

sewerage A system of pipes and treatment plants that collects and cleans sewage (water that contains waste matter produced by human beings).

spillway A passage that allows excess water to flow over or around a dam from a reservoir that is overflowing.

storm drain A drain designed to carry away excess rain and other surface water.

storm surge A sudden onrush of seawater caused by the low atmospheric pressure, high winds, or both effects of such storm systems as hurricanes.

surface runoff Rainwater that runs across the land rather than soaking in.

tributary A stream that flows into a larger stream or river.

tropical To do with the tropics—regions of Earth that lie within about 1,600 miles (2,570 kilometers) north and south of the equator.

tsunami A series of powerful ocean waves produced by an earthquake, landslide, volcanic eruption, or asteroid impact.

upstream Up a river, toward its source.

water cycle (also called the hydrologic cycle) The continuous movement of water as it evaporates from Earth's surface, rises into the air, cools, condenses back into water, and returns to Earth's surface.

water vapor Water in its gaseous state.

BOOKS

Floods, Rev. ed., by Michael Allaby, Facts on File, 2003

Wild Water: Floods, by Tony Allan, Raintree, 2005

Floods and Mudslides: Disaster and Survival, by Bonnie J. Ceban, Enslow Publishers, 2005

Johnstown Flood: The Day the Dam Burst, by Mary Gow, Enslow Publishers, 2003

WEB SITES

http://www.noaa.gov/floods.html

http://www.usgs.gov/hazards/floods/

http://www.nps.gov/jofl/

http://www.tva.gov/river/index.htm

http://www.geoprojects.co.uk/Keyfile/KeyBoscastle.htm

INDEX